Encyclical Letter
of Pope Leo XIII

ON THE
STUDY OF
SACRED SCRIPTURE

Providentissimus Deus

Pauline
BOOKS & MEDIA

BOSTON

N.C.W.C. Translation

ISBN 0-8198-6922-8

Printed and published in the U.S.A. by Pauline Books & Media, 50 St. Paul's Avenue, Boston, MA 02130.

http://www.pauline.org   E-mail: PBM_EDIT@INTERRAMP.COM

Pauline Books & Media is the publishing house of the Daughters of St. Paul, an international congregation of women religious serving the Church with the communications media.

3 4 5 6   99 98 97 96

ENCYCLICAL LETTER
OF POPE LEO XIII

PROVIDENTISSIMUS DEUS

ON THE STUDY OF HOLY SCRIPTURE

To Our Venerable Brethren, All Patriarchs, Primates,
Archbishops, and Bishops of the Catholic World in Grace
and Communion with the Apostolic See

INTRODUCTORY

The God of all Providence, who in the adorable designs of His love at first elevated the human race to the participation of the divine nature, and afterwards delivered it from universal guilt and ruin, restoring it to its primitive dignity, has, in consequence, bestowed upon man a splendid gift and safeguard—making known to him, by supernatural means, the hidden mysteries of His divinity, His wisdom and His mercy. For although in divine revelation there are contained some things which are not beyond the reach of unassisted reason, and which are made the objects of such revelation in order "that all may come to know them with facility, certainty, and safety from error, yet not on this account can supernatural revelation be said to be absolutely necessary; it is only necessary because God has ordained man to a supernatural end."[1] This supernatural revelation, according to the belief of the universal Church, is contained both in unwritten tradition and in written books, which are, therefore, called sacred and canonical because, "being written under the inspiration of the Holy Ghost, they have God for their author, and as such have been delivered to the Church."[2] This belief has been perpetually held and professed by the Church in regard to the books of both Testaments; and there are well known documents of the gravest kind, coming down to us from the earliest times, which proclaim that God, who spoke first by the Prophets, then by His own

---

[1] Conc. Vat. sess. III, cap. ii. *de Revel.*   [2] *Ibid.*

3

mouth, and lastly by the Apostles, composed also the canonical Scripture,[3] and that these are His own oracles and words[4]—a Letter written by our Heavenly Father and transmitted by the sacred writers to the human race in its pilgrimage so far from its heavenly country.[5] If, then, such and so great is the excellence and the dignity of the Scriptures, that God Himself has composed them, and that they treat of God's marvelous mysteries, counsels, and works, it follows that the branch of sacred theology which is concerned with the defence and elucidation of these divine books must be excellent and useful in the highest degree.

Now We, who by the help of God, and not without fruit, have by frequent Letters and exhortation endeavored to promote other branches of study which seemed capable of advancing the glory of God and contributing to the salvation of souls, have for a long time cherished the desire to give an impulse to the noble science of Holy Scripture, and to impart to Scripture study a direction suitable to the needs of the present day. The solicitude of the apostolic office naturally urges and even compels Us, not only to desire that this grand source of Catholic revelation should be made safely and abundantly accessible to the flock of Jesus Christ, but also not to suffer any attempt to defile or corrupt it, either on the part of those who impiously and openly assail the Scriptures, or of those who are led astray into fallacious and imprudent novelties.

We are not ignorant, indeed, Venerable Brethren, that there are not a few Catholics, men of talent and learning, who do devote themselves with ardor to the defence of the sacred writings and to making them better known and understood. But whilst giving to these the commendation they deserve, We cannot but earnestly exhort others also, from whose skill and piety and learning We have a right to expect good results, to give themselves to the same most praiseworthy work. It is Our wish and fervent desire to see an increase in the number of the approved and persevering laborers in the cause of Holy Scripture; and more especially that those whom divine grace has called to Holy Orders, should, day

[3] S. Aug. *de Civ. Dei* xi, 3.
[4] S. Clem. Rom. 1 *ad. Cor.* 45: S. Polycarp. *ad Phil.* 7; S. Iren. *Contra Haereses*, ii, 28, 2.
[5] S. Chrys. *in Gen.* hom. 2, 2; S. Aug. *in Ps.* 30, *serm.*, 2, 1; S. Greg. M. *ad Theod.* ep. iv, 31.

4

by day, as their state demands, display greater diligence and industry in reading, meditating, and explaining it.

I *MOTIVES FOR THE STUDY AND USE OF HOLY SCRIPTURE*

A ITS UTILITY

1. DOCTRINAL.—Among the reasons for which the Holy Scripture is so worthy of commendation—in addition to its own excellence and to the homage which we owe to God's Word—the chief of all is, the innumerable benefits of which it is the source; according to the infallible testimony of the Holy Ghost Himself, who says: "All Scripture is inspired by God and useful for teaching, for reproving, for correcting, for instructing in justice; that the man of God may be perfect, equipped for every good work" (2 Tim. 3:16-17).

a. *Words and Example of Christ.* That such was the purpose of God in giving the Scripture to men is shown by the example of Christ our Lord and of His Apostles. For He Himself who "obtained authority by miracles, merited belief by authority, and by belief drew to Himself the multitude"[6] was accustomed in the exercise of His divine mission, to appeal to the Scriptures. He uses them at times to prove that He is sent by God, and is God Himself. From them He cites instructions for His disciples and confirmation of His doctrine. He vindicates them from the calumnies of objectors; He quotes them against Sadducees and Pharisees and retorts from them upon Satan himself when he dares to tempt Him. At the close of His life His utterances are from the Holy Scripture, and it is the Scripture that He expounds to His disciples after His resurrection, until He ascends to the glory of His Father.

b. *The Apostles.* Faithful to His precepts, the Apostles, although He Himself granted "signs and wonders to be done by their hands" (Acts 14:3), nevertheless used with the greatest effect the sacred writings, in order to persuade the nations everywhere of the wisdom of Christianity, to conquer the obstinacy of the Jews, and to suppress the outbreak of heresy. This is

---

[6] S. Aug. *de Util. Cred.* xiv, 32.

plainly seen in their discourses, especially in those of St. Peter;
these were often little less than a series of citations from the Old
Testament making in the strongest manner for the new dispensa-
tion. We find the same thing in the Gospels of St. Matthew and
St. John and in the Catholic Epistles; and most remarkably of all
in the words of him who "boasts that he learned the law at the
feet of Gamaliel, in order that, being armed with spiritual
weapons, he might afterwards say with confidence, 'the arms of
our warfare are not carnal but mighty unto God.' "[7]

Let all, therefore, especially the novices of the ecclesiastical
army, understand how deeply the sacred books should be es-
teemed, and with what eagerness and reverence they should
approach this great arsenal of heavenly arms. For those whose
duty it is to handle Catholic doctrine before the learned or the
unlearned will nowhere find more ample matter or more abundant
exhortation, whether on the subject of God, the supreme Good
and the all-perfect Being, or of the works which display His
glory and His love. Nowhere is there anything more full or
more express on the subject of the Savior of the world than is to
be found in the whole range of the Bible.

As St. Jerome says, "to be ignorant of the Scripture is not to
know Christ."[8] In its pages His Image stands out, living and
breathing; diffusing everywhere around consolation in trouble,
encouragement to virtue, and attraction to the love of God. And
as to the Church, her institutions, her nature, her office, and her
gifts, we find in Holy Scripture so many references and so many
ready and convincing arguments, that as St. Jerome again most
truly says: "A man who is well grounded in the testimonies of
the Scripture is the bulwark of the Church."[9] And if we come to
morality and discipline, an apostolic man finds in the sacred
writings abundant and excellent assistance; most holy precepts,
gentle and strong exhortation, splendid examples of every virtue,
and finally the promise of eternal reward and the threat of eternal
punishment, uttered in terms of solemn import, in God's name and
in God's own words.

2. ORATORICAL.—And it is this peculiar and singular power
of Holy Scripture, arising from the inspiration of the Holy

[7] S. Hier. *de Stud. Script. ad Paulin.* ep. liii, 3.
[8] *In Isaiam Prol.*　　　　　　　[9] *In Isaiam* 54:12.

Ghost, which gives authority to the sacred orator, fills him with apostolic liberty of speech, and communicates force and power to his eloquence.

a. *Holy Scripture.* For those who infuse into their efforts the spirit and strength of the Word of God speak "not in word only but in power also, and in the Holy Spirit, and in much fulness" (1 Thess. 1:5). Hence, those preachers are foolish and improvident who, in speaking of religion and proclaiming the things of God, use no words but those of human science and human prudence, trusting to their own reasonings rather than to those of God. Their discourses may be brilliant and fine, but they must be feeble and they must be cold, for they are without the fire of the utterance of God[10] and they must fall far short of that mighty power which the speech of God possesses: "for the Word of God is living and effectual, and keener than any two-edged sword; and extending unto the division of the soul and the spirit" (Heb. 4:12). But, indeed, all those who have a right to speak are agreed that there is in the Holy Scripture an eloquence that is wonderfully varied and rich, and worthy of great themes. This St. Augustine thoroughly understood and has abundantly set forth.[11] This, also, is confirmed by the best preachers of all ages, who have gratefully acknowledged that they owed their repute chiefly to the assiduous use of the Bible, and to devout meditation on its pages.

b. *The Fathers.* The holy Fathers well knew all this by practical experience, and they never cease to extol the sacred Scripture and its fruits. In innumerable passages of their writings we find them applying to it such phrases as "an inexhaustible treasury of heavenly doctrine,"[12] or "overflowing fountain of salvation,"[13] or putting it before us as fertile pastures and beautiful gardens in which the flock of the Lord is marvelously refreshed and delighted.[14] Let us listen to the words of St. Jerome, in his Epistle to Nepotian: "Often read the divine Scriptures; yea, let holy reading be always in thy hand; study that

[10] Jerem. 23:29.
[11] *De Doctr. Chr.* iv, 6, 7.
[12] S. Chrys. *in Gen.* Hom. xx, 2; Hom., lx, 3; S. Aug. *de Disc. Christ.* ii.
[13] S. Athan. *Ep. Fest.* xxxix.
[14] S. Aug. *serm.* xxvi, 24; S. Ambr. *in Ps.* 118, *serm.* xix, 2.

which thou thyself must preach.... Let the speech of the priest be ever seasoned with scriptural reading."[15] St. Gregory the Great, than whom no one has more admirably described the pastoral office, writes in the same sense. "Those," he says, "who are zealous in the work of preaching must never cease the study of the written Word of God."[16] St. Augustine, however, warns us that "vainly does the preacher utter the Word of God exteriorly unless he listens to it interiorly;"[17] and St. Gregory instructs sacred orators "first to find in Holy Scripture the knowledge of themselves, and then to carry it to others, lest in reproving others they forget themselves."[18]

Admonitions such as these had, indeed, been uttered long before by the apostolic voice which had learnt its lesson from Christ Himself, who "began to do and teach." It was not to Timothy alone, but to the whole order of the clergy, that the command was addressed: "Take heed to thyself and to thy teaching, be earnest in them. For in so doing thou wilt save both thyself and those who hear thee"(1 Tim. 4:16). For the saving and for the perfection of ourselves and of others there is at hand the very best of help in the Holy Scriptures, as the Book of Psalms, among others, so constantly insists; but those only will find it who bring to this divine reading not only docility and attention but also piety and an innocent life. For the sacred Scripture is not like other books. Dictated by the Holy Spirit, it contains things of the deepest importance, which, in many instances, are most difficult and obscure. To understand and explain such things there is always required the "coming"[19] of the same Holy Spirit; that is to say, His light and His grace; and these, as the Royal Psalmist so frequently insists, are to be sought by humble prayer and guarded by holiness of life.

B PRACTICE OF THE CHURCH

1. EXPRESS LEGISLATION.—It is in this that the watchful care of the Church shines forth conspicuously. By admirable laws and

---

[15] S. Hier. *de Vita Cleric.* ad Nepot.
[16] S. Greg. M., *Regul. past.* ii, 11 (al. 22) ; *Moral.* xvii, 26 (al. 14).
[17] S. Aug. *serm.* clxxix, 1.
[18] S. Greg. M. *Regul. Past,* iii, 24 (*al.* 48).
[19] S. Hier. *in Mich.* 1:10.

regulations, she has always shown herself solicitous that "the celestial treasure of the sacred books, so bountifully bestowed upon man by the Holy Spirit, should not lie neglected."[20] She has prescribed that a considerable portion of them shall be read and piously reflected upon by all her ministers in the daily office of the sacred psalmody. She has ordered that in cathedral churches, in monasteries, and in other convents in which study can conveniently be pursued, they shall be expounded and interpreted by capable men; and she has strictly commanded that her children shall be fed with the saving words of the Gospel at least on Sundays and solemn feasts.[21] Moreover, it is owing to the wisdom and exertions of the Church that there has always been continued, from century to century, that cultivation of Holy Scripture which has been so remarkable and has borne such ample fruit.

2. CONSTANT USE OF THE BIBLE.—And here, in order to strengthen Our teaching and Our exhortations, it is well to recall how, from the beginning of Christianity, all who have been renowned for holiness of life and sacred learning, have given their deep and constant attention to Holy Scripture.

a. *In Early Times.* If we consider the immediate disciples of the Apostles, St. Clement of Rome, St. Ignatius of Antioch, St. Polycarp—or the apologists, such as St. Justin and St. Irenaeus, we find that in their letters and their books, whether in defence of the Catholic Faith or in its commendation, they drew faith, strength, and unction from the Word of God. When there arose, in various sees, catechetical and theological schools, of which the most celebrated were those of Alexandria and of Antioch, there was little taught in those schools but what was contained in the reading, the interpretation, and the defence of the divine written word. From them came forth numbers of Fathers and writers whose laborious studies and admirable writings have justly merited for the three following centuries the appellation of the golden age of biblical exegesis. In the Eastern Church, the greatest name of all is Origen—a man remarkable alike for penetration of genius and for persevering labor; from whose numerous works and his great *Hexapla* almost all have drawn that came after him. Others who have widened the field of this science

---

[20] Conc. Trid. sess. v, *Decret. de reform.*, 1.   [21] *Ibid.* 1-2.

may also be named, as especially eminent; thus, Alexandria could boast of St. Clement and St. Cyril; Palestine, of Eusebius and the other St. Cyril; Cappadocia, of St. Basil the Great and the two St. Gregories, of Nazianzus and Nyssa; Antioch, of St. John Chrysostom, in whom the science of Scripture was rivalled by the splendor of his eloquence. In the Western Church there were many names as great: Tertullian, St. Cyprian, St. Hilary, St. Ambrose, St. Leo the Great, St. Gregory the Great; most famous of all, St. Augustine and St. Jerome, of whom the former was so marvelously acute in penetrating the sense of God's Word and so fertile in the use that he made of it for the promotion of the Catholic truth, and the latter has received from the Church, by reason of his preeminent knowledge of Scripture and his labors in promoting its use, the name, "great Doctor."

b. *In the Middle Ages.*—From this period down to the eleventh century, although biblical studies did not flourish with the same vigor and the same fruitfulness as before, yet they did flourish, and principally by the instrumentality of the clergy. It was their care and solicitude that selected the best and most useful things that the ancients had left, arranged them in order, and published them with additions of their own—as did St. Isidore of Seville, Venerable Bede, and Alcuin, among the most prominent; it was they who illustrated the sacred pages with "glosses" or short commentaries, as we see in Walafrid Strabo and St. Anselm of Laon, or expended fresh labor in securing their integrity, as did St. Peter Damian and Blessed Lanfranc. In the twelfth century many took up, with great success, the allegorical exposition of Scripture. In this kind, St. Bernard is preeminent; and his writings, it may be said, are Scripture all through. With the age of the scholastics came fresh and welcome progress in the study of the Bible. That the scholastics were solicitous about the genuineness of the Latin version is evident from the *Correctoria Biblica,* or lists of emendations, which they have left. But they expended their labors and industry chiefly on interpretation and explanation. To them we owe the accurate and clear distinction, such as had not been given before, of the various senses of the sacred words; the assignment of the value of each "sense" in theology; the division of books into parts, and the summaries of the various parts; the investigation of the objects

of the writers; the demonstration of the connection of sentence
with sentence, and clause with clause; all of which is calculated
to throw much light on the more obscure passages of the sacred
volume. The valuable work of the scholastics in Holy Scripture
is seen in their theological treatises and in their Scripture commentaries; and in this respect the greatest name among them all
is St. Thomas Aquinas.

c.—*In Modern Times.*—When Our predecessor, Clement V.,
established chairs of Oriental literature in the Roman College and
in the principal universities of Europe, Catholics began to make
more accurate investigation on the original text of the Bible as
well as on the Latin version. The revival amongst us of Greek
learning, and, much more, the happy invention of the art of print-
ing, gave a strong impetus to biblical studies. In a brief space
of time, innumerable editions, especially of the Vulgate, poured
from the press and were diffused throughout the Catholic world;
so honored and loved was Holy Scripture during that very period
against which the enemies of the Church direct their calumnies.
Nor must we forget how many learned men there were, chiefly
among the religious orders, who did excellent work for the Bible
between the Council of Vienne and that of Trent; men who, by
the employment of modern means and appliances, and by the
tribute of their own genius and learning, not only added to the
rich stores of ancient times but prepared the way for the suc-
ceeding century, the century which followed the Council of Trent,
when it almost seemed that the great age of the Fathers had re-
turned. For it is well known, and We recall it with pleasure, that
Our predecessors, from Pius IV. to Clement VIII. caused to be
prepared the celebrated editions of the Vulgate and the Sep-
tuagint, which, having been published by the command and
authority of Sixtus V. and of the same Clement, are now in com-
mon use. At this time, moreover, were carefully brought out
various other ancient versions of the Bible, and the Polyglots
of Antwerp and of Paris, most important for the investigation
of the true meaning of the text; nor is there any one book of
either Testament which did not find more than one expositor,
nor any grave question which did not profitably exercise the
ability of many inquirers, among whom there are not a few—
more especially of those who made most use of the Fathers—

who have acquired great reputation. From that time downwards the labor and solicitude of Catholics has never been wanting; for as time went on, eminent scholars have carried on biblical study with success, and have defended Holy Scripture against *rationalism* with the same weapons of philology and kindred sciences with which it had been attacked. The calm and fair consideration of what has been said will clearly show that the Church has never failed in taking due measures to bring the Scriptures within reach of her children, and that she has ever held fast and exercised profitably that guardianship conferred upon her by Almighty God for the protection and glory of His holy Word; so that she has never required, nor does she now require, any stimulation from without.

II *PLAN FOR THE STUDY OF HOLY SCRIPTURE.*

A OUR ADVERSARIES

We must now, Venerable Brethren, as Our purpose demands, impart to you such counsels as seem best suited for carrying on successfully the study of biblical science.

But first it must be clearly understood whom we have to oppose and contend against, and what are their tactics and their arms. In earlier times the contest was chiefly with those who, relying on private judgment and repudiating the divine traditions and teaching office of the Church, held the Scriptures to be the one source of revelation and the final appeal in matters of faith. Now, we have to meet the Rationalists, true children and inheritors of the older heretics, who, trusting in their turn to their own way of thinking, have rejected even the scraps and remnants of Christian belief which had been handed down to them. They deny that there is any such thing as revelation or inspiration, or Holy Scriptures at all; they see, instead, only the forgeries and the falsehoods of men; they set down the Scripture narratives as stupid fables and lying stories: the prophecies and the oracles of God are to them either predictions made up after the event or forecasts formed by the light of nature; the miracles and the wonders of God's power are not what they are said to be, but the startling effects of natural law, or else mere tricks and myths;

and the apostolic Gospels and writings are not the work of the Apostles at all.

These detestable errors, whereby they think they destroy the truth of the divine books, are obtruded on the world as the peremptory pronouncements of a certain newly-invented "free science," a science, however, which is so far from final that they are perpetually modifying and supplementing it. And there are some of them who, notwithstanding their impious opinions and utterances about God, and Christ, the Gospels and the rest of Holy Scripture, would fain be considered both theologians and Christians, and men of the gospel, and who attempt to disguise by such honorable name their rashness and their pride. To them we must add not a few professors of other sciences who approve their views and give them assistance and are urged to attack the Bible by a similar intolerance of revelation. And it is deplorable to see these attacks growing every day more numerous and more severe. It is sometimes men of learning and judgment who are assailed; but these have little difficulty in defending themselves from evil consequences.

The efforts and the arts of the enemy are chiefly directed against the more ignorant masses of the people. They diffuse their deadly poison by means of books, pamphlets, and newspapers; they spread it by addresses and by conversation; they are found everywhere; and they are in possession of numerous schools, taken by violence from the Church, in which, by ridicule and scurrilous jesting, they pervert the credulous and unformed minds of the young to the contempt of Holy Scripture. Should not these things, Venerable Brethren, stir up and set on fire the heart of every pastor, so that to this "so-called knowledge" (1 Tim. 6:20), may be opposed the ancient and true science which the Church, through the Apostles, has received from Christ, and that Holy Scripture may find the champions that are needed in so momentous a battle?

B PREPARATORY COURSE OF STUDIES

1. PROFESSORS.—Let our first care, then, be to see that in seminaries and academical institutions the study of Holy Scripture be placed on such a footing as its own importance and the

circumstances of the time demand. With this view, the first thing which requires attention is the wise choice of professors. Teachers of sacred Scripture are not to be appointed at haphazard out of the crowd; but they must be men whose character and fitness are proved by their love of, and their long familiarity with the Bible, and by suitable learning and study.

It is a matter of equal importance to provide in time for a continuous succession of such teachers; and it will be well, wherever this can be done, to select young men of good promise who have successfully accomplished their theological course, and to set them apart exclusively for Holy Scripture, affording them facilities for full and complete studies. Professors, thus chosen and thus prepared may enter with confidence on the task that is appointed for them; and that they may carry out their work well and profitably, let them take heed to the instructions We now proceed to give.

2. PREPARATORY STUDIES.—At the commencement of the course of Holy Scripture let the professor strive earnestly to form the judgment of the young beginners so as to train them equally to defend the sacred writings and to penetrate their meaning. This is the object of the treatise which is called "Introduction." Here the student is taught how to prove the integrity and authority of the Bible, how to investigate and ascertain its true sense, and how to meet and refute objections. It is needless to insist upon the importance of making these preliminary studies in an orderly and thorough fashion, with the accompaniment and assistance of theology; for the whole subsequent course must rest on the foundation thus laid and make use of the light thus acquired. Next, the teacher will turn his earnest attention to that more fruitful division of Scripture science which has to do with interpretation, wherein is imparted the method of using the Word of God for the advantage of religion and piety. We recognize, without hesitation, that neither the extent of the matter nor the time at disposal allows each single book of the Bible to be separately gone through. But the teaching should result in a definite and ascertained method of interpretation—and, therefore, the professor should equally avoid the mistake of giving a mere taste of every book, and of dwelling at too great length on

14

a part of one book. If most schools cannot do what is done in the large institutions—that is, take the students through the whole of one or two books continuously and with a certain development—yet at least those parts which are selected should be treated with suitable fullness; in such a way that the students may learn from the sample that is thus put before them to love and use the remainder of the sacred book during the whole of their lives.

3. TEXT.—The professor, following the tradition of antiquity, will make use of the Vulgate as his text; for the Council of Trent decreed that "in public lectures, disputations, preaching, and exposition,"[22] the Vulgate is the "authentic" version; and this is the existing custom of the Church. At the same time, the other versions, which Christian antiquity has approved, should not be neglected, more especially the more ancient MSS. For, although the meaning of the Hebrew and Greek is substantially rendered by the Vulgate, nevertheless, wherever there may be ambiguity or want of clearness, the "examination of older tongues,"[23] to quote St. Augustine, will be useful and advantageous. But in this matter we need hardly say that the greatest prudence is required, for the "office of a commentator," as St. Jerome says, "is to set forth not what he himself would prefer, but what his author says."[24] The question of "reading" having been, when necessary, carefully discussed, the next thing is to investigate and expound the meaning. And the first counsel to be given is this: that the more our adversaries contend to the contrary, so much the more solicitously should we adhere to the received and approved canons of interpretation. Hence, whilst weighing the meanings of words, the connection of ideas, the parallelism of passages, and the like, we should by all means make use of such illustrations as can be drawn from apposite erudition of an external sort; but this should be done with caution, so as not to bestow on questions of this kind more labor and time than are spent on the sacred books themselves, and not to overload the minds of the students with a mass of information that will be rather a hindrance than a help.

[22] Sess. iv, *Decr. de Edit. et Usu Sacr. Libr.*
[23] *De Doctr. Chr.* iii, 4.
[24] *Ad Pammachium.*

The professor may now safely pass on to the use of Scripture in matters of theology. On this head it must be observed that, in addition to the usual reasons which make ancient writings more or less difficult to understand, there are some which are peculiar to the Bible. For the language of the Bible is employed to express, under the inspiration of the Holy Spirit, many things which are beyond the power and scope of the reason of man— that is to say, divine mysteries and all that is related to them. There is sometimes in such passages a fullness and a hidden depth of meaning which the letter hardly expresses and which the laws of interpretation hardly warrant. Moreover, the literal sense itself frequently admits other senses, adapted to illustrate dogma or to confirm morality.

1.   GUIDES.—Wherefore, it must be recognized that the sacred writings are wrapt in a certain religious obscurity, and that no one can enter into their interior without a guide;[25] God so dis- posing, as the holy Fathers commonly teach, in order that men may investigate them with greater ardor and earnestness, and that what is attained with difficulty may sink more deeply into the mind and heart, and, most of all, that they may understand that God has delivered the Holy Scripture to the Church, and that in reading and making use of His Word, they must follow the Church as their guide and their teacher. St. Irenaeus long since laid down, that where the *charismata* of God were, there the truth was to be learned, and the Holy Scripture was safely in- terpreted by those who had the apostolic succession.[26]

a.   *The Church.*—His teaching, and that of other holy Fathers, is taken up by the Council of the Vatican, which in renewing the decree of Trent declares its "mind" to be this—that "in things of faith and morals, belonging to the building up of Christian doc- trine, that is to be considered the true sense of Holy Scripture, which has been held and is held by our Holy Mother the Church, whose place it is to judge of the true sense and interpretation of the Scriptures; and, therefore, that it is permitted to no one to interpret Holy Scripture against such sense or also against the

[25] S. Hier. *ad Paulin. de Studio Script.* ep. liii, 4.
[26] *Contra Haereses*, iv, 26, 5.

16

unanimous agreement of the Fathers."[27] By this most wise decree the Church by no means prevents or restrains the pursuit of biblical science, but rather protects it from error, and largely assists its real progress.

A wide field is still left open to the private student, in which his hermeneutical skill may display itself with signal effect and to the advantage of the Church. On the one hand, in those passages of Holy Scripture, which have not as yet received a certain and definite interpretation, such labors may, in the benignant providence of God, prepare for and bring to maturity the judgment of the Church; on the other, in passages already defined the private student may do work equally valuable, either by setting them forth more clearly to the flock and more skillfully to scholars, or by defending them more powerfully from hostile attack. Wherefore the first and dearest object of the Catholic commentator should be to interpret those passages which have received an authentic interpretation either from the sacred writers themselves, under the inspiration of the Holy Spirit (as in many places of the New Testament), or from the Church, under the assistance of the same Holy Spirit, whether by her solemn judgment or her ordinary and universal *magisterium*[28]— to interpret these passages in that identical sense, and to prove by all the resources of science, that sound hermeneutical laws admit of no other interpretation.

b. *Analogy of Faith.*—In the other passages the analogy of faith should be followed, and Catholic doctrine, as authoritatively proposed by the Church, should be held as the supreme law; for seeing that the same God is the author both of the sacred books and of the doctrine committed to the Church, it is clearly impossible that any teaching can, by legitimate means, be extracted from the former, which shall, in any respect, be at variance with the latter. Hence it follows that all interpretation is foolish and false which either makes the sacred writers disagree one with another, or is opposed to the doctrine of the Church.

c. *The Fathers.*—The professor of Holy Scripture, therefore, amongst other recommendations, must be well acquainted with

---

[27] Sess. iii, cap. ii, *de Revel;* cf. Conc. Trid, sess. iv, *Decret. de Edit. et Usu Sacr. libr.*

[28] Conc. Vat. sess. III, cap. ii, *de Fide.*

the whole circle of theology and deeply read in the commentaries
of the holy Fathers and Doctors, and other interpreters of
mark.[29] This is inculcated by St. Jerome, and still more frequently by St. Augustine, who thus justly complains: "If there
is no branch of teaching, however humble and easy to learn, which
does not require a master, what can be a greater sign of rashness
and pride than to refuse to study the books of the divine mysteries by the help of those who have interpreted them?"[30] The
other Fathers have said the same, and have confirmed it by their
example, for they "endeavored to acquire the understanding of
the Holy Scriptures not by their own lights and ideas, but from
the writings and authority of the ancients, who, in their turn,
as we know, received the rule of interpretation in direct line from
the Apostles."[31] The holy Fathers "to whom, after the Apostles,
the Church owes its growth—who have planted, watered, built,
governed, and cherished it,"[32] the holy Fathers, We say, are of
supreme authority, whenever they all interpret in one and the
same manner any text of the Bible, as pertaining to the doctrine
of faith or morals; for their unanimity clearly evinces that such
interpretation has come down from the Apostles as a matter of
Catholic faith. The opinion of the Fathers is also of very great
weight when they treat of these matters in their capacity of
Doctors unofficially; not only because they excel in their knowledge of revealed doctrine and in their acquaintance with many
things which are useful in understanding the apostolic books,
but because they are men of eminent sanctity and of ardent zeal
for the truth, on whom God has bestowed a more ample measure
of His light. Wherefore the expositor should make it his duty to
follow their footsteps with all reverence, and to use their labors
with intelligent appreciation.

d. *Later Commentators.*—But he must not on that account
consider that it is forbidden, when just cause exists, to push
inquiry and exposition beyond what the Fathers have done; provided he carefully observes the rule so wisely laid down by St
Augustine—not to depart from the literal and obvious sense, except only where reason makes it untenable or necessity requires;[33]

[29] *Ibid.* 6, 7.
[30] *De Util. Cred.* xvii, 35.
[31] Rufinus *Hist. Eccl.* ii, 9.
[32] S. Aug. *c. Julian.* ii, 10, 37.
[33] *De Gen. ad Litt.* viii, 7, 13.

a rule to which it is the more necessary to adhere strictly in these
times, when the thirst for novelty and unrestrained freedom of
thought make the danger of error most real and proximate.
Neither should those passages be neglected which the Fathers
have understood in an allegorical or figurative sense, more especially when such interpretation is justified by the literal, and
when it rests on the authority of many. For this method of
interpretation has been received by the Church from the Apostles
and has been approved by her own practice, as the holy Liturgy
attests; although it is true that the holy Fathers did not thereby pretend directly to demonstrate dogmas of faith, but used it
as a means of promoting virtue and piety, such as, by their own
experience, they knew to be most valuable.

The authority of other Catholic interpreters is not so great;
but the study of the Scriptures has always continued to advance
in the Church, and, therefore, these commentaries also have their
own honorable place, and are serviceable in many ways for the
refutation of assailants and the explanation of difficulties. But
it is most unbecoming to pass by, in ignorance or contempt, the
excellent work which Catholics have left in abundance, and to
have recourse to the works of non-Catholics—and to seek in
them, to the detriment of sound doctrine and often to the peril
of faith, the explanation of passages on which Catholics long ago
have successfully employed their talent and their labor. For
although the studies of non-Catholics, used with prudence, may
sometimes be of use to the Catholic student, he should, nevertheless, bear well in mind—as the Fathers also teach in numerous
passages[34]—that the sense of Holy Scripture can nowhere be
found incorrupt outside the Church, and cannot be expected to be
found in writers who, being without the true faith, only gnaw
the bark of the sacred Scripture, and never attain its pith.

2. HOLY SCRIPTURE AND THEOLOGY.—Most desirable is it, and
most essential, that the whole teaching of theology should be
pervaded and animated by the use of the divine Word of God.
This is what the Fathers and the greatest theologians of all ages
have desired and reduced to practice. It was chiefly out of the
sacred writings that they endeavored to proclaim and establish

[34] Cf. Clem. Alex. *Strom.* vii, 16; Orig. *de Princ.* iv, 8; *in Lec.* hom.
4, 8; Tert., *de Praes.* 15; *S. Hilar. Pict. in Matt.* 13:1.

the Articles of Faith and the truths connected with it, and it was
in them, together with divine tradition, that they found the refutation of heretical error, and the reasonableness, the true meaning, and the mutual relation of the truths of Catholicism. Nor
will any one wonder at this who considers that the sacred books
hold such an eminent position among the sources of revelation
that without their assiduous study and use, theology cannot be
placed on its true footing, or treated as its dignity demands

For although it is right and proper that students in academies
and schools should be chiefly exercised in acquiring a scientific
knowledge of dogma, by means of reasoning from the Articles of
Faith to their consequences, according to the rules of approved
and sound philosophy—nevertheless the judicious and instructed
theologian will by no means pass by that method of doctrinal
demonstration which draws its proof from the authority of the
Bible; "for theology does not receive her first principles from any
other science, but immediately from God by revelation. And,
therefore, she does not receive of other sciences as from a su-
perior, but uses them as her inferiors or handmaids."[35] It is this
view of doctrinal teaching which is laid down and recommended
by the prince of theologians, St. Thomas of Aquin;[36] who, moreover, shows—such being the essential character of Christian
theology—how she can defend her own principles against attack:
"If the adversary," he says, "do but grant any portion of the
divine revelation, we have an argument against him; thus,
against a heretic we can employ Scripture authority, and against
those who deny one article, we can use another. But if our op-
ponent reject divine revelation entirely, there is then no way
left to prove the Articles of Faith by reasoning; we can only
solve the difficulties which are raised against them."[37] Care must
be taken, then, that beginners approach the study of the Bible
well prepared and furnished; otherwise, just hopes will be frus-
trated, or, perchance, what is worse, they will unthinkingly risk
the danger of error, falling an easy prey to the sophisms and
labored erudition of the Rationalists. The best preparation will
be a conscientious application to philosophy and theology under

[35] S. Greg. M. *Moral.* xx, 9 (al. 11).
[36] *Summ. theol.* p. i, q. i, a. 5, ad 2.
[37] *Ibid.* a. 8.

20

the guidance of St. Thomas of Aquin, and a thorough training therein—as We Ourselves have elsewhere pointed out and directed. By this means, both in biblical studies and in that part of theology which is called *positive,* they will pursue the right path and make satisfactory progress.

D DEFENCE OF THE AUTHORITY OF HOLY SCRIPTURE

1. THE WORK OF THE CHURCH.—To prove, to expound, to illustrate Catholic doctrine by legitimate and skillful interpretation of the Bible is much; but there is a second part of the object of equal importance and equal difficulty—the maintenance in the strongest possible way of its full authority. This cannot be done completely or satisfactorily except by means of the living and proper *magisterium* of the Church. The Church, "by reason of her wonderful propagation, her distinguished sanctity and inexhaustible fecundity in good, her Catholic unity, and her unshaken stability, is herself a great and perpetual motive of credibility, and an unassailable testimony to her own divine mission."[38] But since the divine and infallible *magisterium* of the Church rests also on the authority of Holy Scripture, the first thing to be done is to vindicate the trustworthiness of the sacred records, at least as human documents, from which can be clearly proved, as from primitive and authentic testimony, the divinity and mission of Christ our Lord, the institution of a hierarchical Church, and the primacy of Peter and his successors. It is most desirable, therefore, that there should be numerous members of the clergy well prepared to enter upon a contest of this nature, and to repulse hostile assaults, chiefly trusting in that armor of God recommended by the Apostle (Eph. 6:13-17), but also not unaccustomed to modern methods of attack.

This is beautifully alluded to by St. John Chrysostom, when describing the duties of priests:

We must use every endeavor that the "Word of God may dwell in us abundantly" (Col. 3:16); not merely for one kind of fight must we be prepared—for the contest is many-sided and the enemy is of every sort; and they do not all use the same weapons nor make their onset in the same way. Wherefore it is needful that the man who has to

[38] Conc. Vat. sess. III, c. iii, *de Fide.*

contend against all should be acquainted with the engines and the arts of all—that he should be at once archer and slinger, commandant and officer, general and private soldier, foot-soldier and horseman, skilled in sea-fight and in siege; for, unless he knows every trick and turn of war, the devil is well able, if only a single door be left open, to get in his fierce bands and carry off the sheep.[39]

2. Equipment of the Defenders.—The sophisms of the enemy and his manifold arts of attack we have already touched upon. Let Us now say a word of advice on the means of defence.

a. *Oriental Languages.* The first means is the study of the Oriental languages and of the art of criticism. These two acquirements are in these days held in high estimation, and, therefore, the clergy, by making themselves more or less fully acquainted with them as time and place may demand, will the better be able to discharge their office with becoming credit; for they must make themselves "all things to men" (1 Cor. 9:22), always "ready with an answer to everyone who asks a reason for the hope that is in you" (1 Peter 3:15). Hence it is most proper that professors of sacred Scripture and theologians should master those tongues in which the sacred books were originally written; and it would be well that ecclesiastical students also should cultivate them, more especially those who aspire to academic degrees. And endeavors should be made to establish in all academic institutions—as has already been laudably done in many—chairs of the other ancient languages, especially the Semitic, and of subjects connected therewith, for the benefit, principally, of those who are intended to profess sacred literature. These latter, with a similar object in view, make themselves well and thoroughly acquainted with the art of true criticism.

There has arisen, to the great detriment of religion, an inept method, dignified by the name of the "higher criticism," which pretends to judge of the origin, integrity, and authority of each book from internal indications alone. It is clear, on the other hand, that in historical questions, such as the origin and the handing down of writings, the witness of history is of primary importance, and that historical investigation should be made with the utmost care; and that in this matter internal evidence is

[39] *De Sacerdotio* iv, 4.

22

seldom of great value, except as confirmation. To look upon it
in any other light will be to open the door to many evil consequences. It will make the enemies of religion much more bold
and confident in attacking and mangling the sacred books; and
this vaunted "higher criticism" will resolve itself into the re-
flection of the bias and the prejudice of the critics. It will not
throw on the Scripture the light which is sought, or prove of any
advantage to doctrine; it will only give rise to disagreement and
dissension, those sure notes of error, which the critics in question
so plentifully exhibit in their own persons; and seeing that most
of them are tainted with false philosophy and rationalism, it
must lead to the elimination from the sacred writings of all
prophecy and miracles, and of everything else that is outside the
natural order.

b. *Natural Sciences.*—In the second place, we have to contend
against those who, making an evil use of physical science, minute-
ly scrutinize the sacred book in order to detect the writers in a
mistake, and to take occasion to vilify its contents. Attacks of
this kind, bearing as they do on matters of sensible experience,
are peculiarly dangerous to the masses, and also to the young
who are beginning their literary studies; for the young, if they
lose their reverence for the Holy Scripture on one or more points,
are easily led to give up believing in it altogether.

It need not be pointed out how the nature of science, just as
it is so admirably adapted to show forth the glory of the Great
Creator, provided it be taught as it should be, so, if it be per-
versely imparted to the youthful intelligence, it may prove most
fatal in destroying the principles of true philosophy and in the
corruption of morality. Hence, to the professor of sacred Scripture a knowledge of natural science will be of very great assistance in detecting such attacks on the sacred books, and in refut-
ing them. There can never, indeed, be any real discrepancy between the theologian and the physicist, as long as each confines
himself within his own lines, and both are careful, as St. Augustine warns us, "not to make rash assertions, or to assert what is
not known as known."[40] If dissension should arise between them,

---

[40] *In Gen. op. Imperf.* ix, 30.

here is the rule also laid down by St. Augustine for the theologian:

Whatever they can really demonstrate to be true of physical nature we must show to be capable of reconciliation with our Scriptures; and whatever they assert in their treatises, which is contrary to these Scriptures of ours, that is to Catholic faith, we must either prove it as well as we can to be entirely false, or at all events we must, without the smallest hesitation, believe it to be so.[41]

To understand how just is the rule here formulated we must remember, first, that the sacred writers, or to speak more accurately, the Holy Spirit "who spoke by them, did not intend to teach men these things (that is to say, the essential nature of the things of the visible universe), things in no way profitable unto salvation."[42] Hence they did not seek to penetrate the secrets of nature, but rather described and dealt with things in more or less figurative language, or in terms which were commonly used at the time, and which in many instances are daily used at this day, even by the most eminent men of science. Ordinary speech primarily and properly describes what comes under the senses; and somewhat in the same way the sacred writers—as the Angelic Doctor also reminds us—"went by what sensibly appeared,"[43] or put down what God, speaking to men, signified, in the way men could understand and were accustomed to.

The unshrinking defence of the Holy Scripture, however, does not require that we should equally uphold all the opinions which each of the Fathers or the more recent interpreters have put forth in explaining it; for it may be that, in commenting on passages where physical matters occur, they have sometimes expressed the ideas of their own times, and thus made statements which in these days have been abandoned as incorrect. Hence, in their interpretations, we must carefully note what they lay down as belonging to faith, or as intimately connected with faith —what they are unanimous in. For "in those things which do not come under the obligation of faith, the saints were at liberty to hold divergent opinions, just as we ourselves are,"[44] according

41 *De Gen. ad Litt.*, i, 21, 41.
42 S. Aug. *ib.* 9, 20.
43 *Summa Theol.* p. i, q. lxxx, a. 1, ad 3.
44 *In Sent.* ii, Dist. q. i, a. 3.

24

to the saying of St. Thomas. And in another place he says most admirably:

When philosophers are agreed upon a point, and it is not contrary to our faith, it is safer, in my opinion, neither to lay down such a point as a dogma of faith, even though it is perhaps so presented by the philosophers, nor to reject it as against faith, lest we thus give to the wise of this world an occasion of despising our faith.[45]

The Catholic interpreter, although he should show that those facts of natural science which investigators affirm to be now quite certain are not contrary to the Scripture rightly explained, must, nevertheless, always bear in mind, that much which has been held and proved as certain has afterwards been called in question and rejected. And if writers on physics travel outside the boundaries of their own branch, and carry their erroneous teaching into the domain of philosophy, let them be handed over to philosophers for refutation.

c. *History.*—The principles here laid down will apply to cognate sciences, and especially to history. It is a lamentable fact that there are many who with great labor carry out and publish investigations on the monuments of antiquity, the manners and institutions of nations, and other illustrative subjects, and whose chief purpose in all this is too often to find mistakes in the sacred writings and so to shake and weaken their authority. Some of these writers display not only extreme hostility, but the greatest unfairness; in their eyes a profane book or ancient document is accepted without hesitation, whilst the Scripture, if they only find in it a suspicion of error, is set down with the slightest possible discussion as quite untrustworthy. It is true, no doubt, that copyists have made mistakes in the text of the Bible; this question, when it arises, should be carefully considered on its merits, and the fact not too easily admitted, but only in those passages where the proof is clear.

3. INERRANCY OF HOLY SCRIPTURE.—It may also happen that the sense of a passage remains ambiguous, and in this case good hermeneutical methods will greatly assist in clearing up the obscurity. But it is absolutely wrong and forbidden either to narrow inspiration to certain parts only of Holy Scripture or to ad-

[45] *Opusc.* x.

mit that the sacred writer has erred. As to the system of those
who, in order to rid themselves of these difficulties, do not hesitate to concede that divine inspiration regards the things of
faith and morals, and nothing beyond, because (as they wrongly
think) in a question of the truth or falsehood of a passage we
should consider not so much what God has said as the reason
and purpose which He had in mind in saying it—this system
cannot be tolerated.

a. *Extent of Inspiration.*—For all the books which the Church
receives as sacred and canonical are written wholly and entirely,
with all their parts, at the dictation of the Holy Spirit; and so
far is it from being possible that any error can coexist with inspiration, that inspiration not only is essentially incompatible
with error, but excludes and rejects it as absolutely and neces-
sarily as it is impossible that God Himself, the supreme Truth,
can utter that which is not true. This is the ancient and un-
changing faith of the Church, solemnly defined in the Councils of
Florence and of Trent, and finally confirmed and more expressly
formulated by the Council of the Vatican. These are the words
of the last:

The books of the Old and New Testament, whole and entire, with
all their parts, as enumerated in the decree of the same Council
(Trent) and in the ancient Latin Vulgate, are to be received as sacred
and canonical. And the Church holds them as sacred and canonical
not because, having been composed by human industry, they were
afterwards approved by her authority; nor only because they contain
revelation without errors, but because, having been written under the
inspiration of the Holy Spirit, they have God for their Author.[46]

Hence, because the Holy Spirit employed men as his instru-
ments, we cannot, therefore, say that it was these inspired instru-
ments who, perchance, have fallen into error, and not the primary
author. For, by supernatural power, He so moved and impelled
them to write—He so assisted them when writing—that the things
which He ordered, and those only, they, first, rightly understood,
then willed faithfully to write down, and finally expressed in apt
words and with infallible truth. Otherwise, it could not be said
that He was the Author of the entire Scripture. Such has always

[46] Sess. III, cap. ii, *de Rev.*

26

been the persuasion of the Fathers. "Therefore," says St. Augustine, "since they wrote the things which He showed and uttered to them, it cannot be pretended that He is not the writer; for His members executed what their head dictated."[47]   And St. Gregory the Great thus pronounces: "Most superfluous it is to inquire who wrote these things—we loyally believe the Holy Spirit to be the author of the book. He wrote it who dictated it for writing; He wrote it who inspired its execution."[48]

b.   *Inspiration Incompatible with Error.*—It follows that those who maintain that an error is possible in any genuine passage of the sacred writings either pervert the Catholic notion of inspiration or make God the author of such error. And so emphatically were all the Fathers and Doctors agreed that the divine writings, as left by the hagiographers, are free from all error, that they labored earnestly, with no less skill than reverence, to reconcile with each other those numerous passages which seem at variance—the very passages which in great measure have been taken up by the "higher criticism;" for they were unanimous in laying it down that those writings, in their entirety and in all their parts were equally from the *afflatus* of Almighty God, and that God, speaking by the sacred writers, could not set down anything but what was true. The words of St. Augustine to St. Jerome may sum up what they taught:

On my own part I confess to your charity that it is only to those books of Scripture which are now called canonical that I have learned to pay such honor and reverence as to believe most firmly that none of their writers has fallen into any error. And if in these books I meet anything which seems contrary to truth, I shall not hesitate to conclude either that the text is faulty, or that the translator has not expressed the meaning of the passage, or that I myself do not understand.[49]

4.   COOPERATION OF CATHOLIC SCHOLARS.—But to undertake fully and perfectly, and with all the weapons of the best science, the defence of the Holy Bible is far more than can be looked for from the exertions of commentators and theologians alone. It is an enterprise in which we have a right to expect the cooperation

[47] *De Consensu Evangel.* i, 35.
[48] *Praef. in Job,* n. 2.
[49] *Ep. lxxxii,* 1, et alibi.

of all those Catholics who have acquired reputation in any branch
of learning whatever. As in the past, so at the present time, the
Church is never without the graceful support of her accomplished
children; may their services to the Faith grow and increase!
For there is nothing which We believe to be more needful than
that truth should find defenders more powerful and more numerous than the enemies it has to face; nor is there anything
which is better calculated to impress the masses with respect
for truth than to see it boldly proclaimed by learned and distinguished men.

Moreover, the bitter tongues of objectors will be silenced or at
least they will not dare to insist so shamelessly that faith is the
enemy of science, when they see that scientific men of eminence
in their profession show towards faith the most marked honor
and respect. Seeing, then, that those can do so much for the
advantage of religion on whom the goodness of Almighty God has
bestowed, together with the grace of the faith, great natural
talent, let such men, in this bitter conflict of which the Holy
Scripture is the object, select each of them the branch of study
most suitable to his circumstances, and endeavor to excel therein,
and thus be prepared to repulse with credit and distinction the
assaults on the Word of God. And it is Our pleasing duty to give
deserved praise to a work which certain Catholics have taken up
—that is to say, the formation of societies and the contribution
of considerable sums of money, for the purpose of supplying
studious and learned men with every kind of help and assistance
in carrying out complete studies. Truly an excellent manner of
investing money, and well suited to the times in which we live!
The less hope of public patronage there is for Catholic study, the
more ready and the more abundant should be the liberality of
private persons—those to whom God has given riches thus will-
ingly making use of their means to safeguard the treasure of His
revealed doctrine.

5. DIRECTIVE NORM FOR SCHOLARS.—In order that all these
endeavors and exertions may really prove advantageous to the
cause of the Bible, let scholars keep steadfastly to the principles
which We have in this letter laid down. Let them loyally hold
that God, the Creator and Ruler of all things, is also the Author

of the Scriptures—and that, therefore, nothing can be proved
either by physical science or archaeology which can really contra-
dict the Scriptures. If, then, apparent contradiction be met with,
every effort should be made to remove it. Judicious theologians
and commentators should be consulted as to what is the true or
most probable meaning of the passage in discussion and the
hostile arguments should be carefully weighed. Even if the
difficulty is after all not cleared up and the discrepancy seems to
remain, the contest must not be abandoned; truth cannot contra-
dict truth, and we may be sure that some mistake has been made
either in the interpretation of the sacred words or in the polemic
discussion itself; and if no such mistake can be detected, we
must then suspend judgment for the time being.

There have been objections without number perseveringly
directed against the Scripture for many a long year, which have
been proved to be futile and are now never heard of; and not
unfrequently interpretations have been placed on certain passages of Scripture (not belonging to the rule of faith or morals)
which have been rectified by more careful investigations. As
time goes on, mistaken views die and disappear; but "truth
remaineth and groweth stronger forever and ever (3 Esdr. 4:38).
Wherefore, as no one should be so presumptuous as to think that
he understands the whole of the Scripture, in which St. Augustine himself confessed that there was more that he did not know,
than that he knew,[50] so, if he should come upon anything that
seems incapable of solution, he must take to heart the cautious
rule of the same holy Doctor: "It is better even to be oppressed
by unknown but useful signs, than to interpret them uselessly
and thus to throw off the yoke only to be caught in the trap of
error."[51]

As to those who pursue the subsidiary studies of which We
have spoken, if they honestly and modestly follow the counsels
We have given—if by their pen and their voice they make their
studies profitable against the enemies of truth, and useful in
saving the young from the loss of their faith—they may justly
congratulate themselves on their worthy service to the sacred
writings, and on affording to Catholicism that assistance which

[50] *Ad Ianuar.* ep. lv, 21.   [51] *De Doct. Chr.* iii, 9, 18.

the Church has a right to expect from the piety and learning of her children.

CONCLUSION

Such, Venerable Brethren, are the admonitions and the instructions which, by the help of God, We have thought it well, at the present moment, to offer to you on the study of Holy Scripture. It will now be your province to see that what We have said be observed and put in practice with all due reverence and exactness; that so We may prove Our gratitude to God for the communication to man of the words of His wisdom, and that all the good results so much to be desired may be realized, especially as they affect the training of the students of the Church, which is Our own great solicitude and the Church's hope.

Exert yourselves with willing alacrity, and use your authority and your persuasion in order that these studies may be held in just regard and may flourish in seminaries and in the educational institutions which are under your jurisdiction. Let them flourish in completeness and in happy success, under the direction of the Church, in accordance with the salutary teaching and example of the holy Fathers, and the laudable traditions of antiquity; and, as time goes on, let them be widened and extended as the interests and glory of truth may require—the interest of that Catholic truth which comes from above, the never-failing source of man's salvation. Finally, We admonish, with paternal love, all students and ministers of the Church always to approach the sacred writings with reverence and piety; for it is impossible to attain to the profitable understanding thereof unless the arrogance of "earthly" science be laid aside, and there be excited in the heart the holy desire for that wisdom "which is from above." In this way the intelligence, which is once admitted to these sacred studies, and thereby illuminated and strengthened, will acquire a marvelous facility in detecting and avoiding the fallacies of human science, and in gathering and using for eternal salvation all that is valuable and precious; whilst, at the same time, the heart will grow warm, and will strive, with ardent longing, to advance in virtue and in divine love. "Blessed are they who examine His testimonies; they shall seek Him with their whole heart" (Ps. 18:2).

30

And now, filled with hope in the divine assistance, and trusting to your pastoral solicitude—as a pledge of heavenly grace, and a sign of Our special good-will—to you all, and to the clergy, and the whole flock entrusted to you, We lovingly impart in Our Lord the Apostolic Benediction.

Given at St. Peter's, at Rome, the 18th day of November, 1893, the sixteenth year of Our Pontificate.

POPE LEO XIII.

ALASKA
750 West 5th Ave., Anchorage, AK 99501; 907-272-8183

CALIFORNIA
3908 Sepulveda Blvd., Culver City, CA 90230; 310-397-8676
5945 Balboa Ave., San Diego, CA 92111; 619-565-9181
46 Geary Street, San Francisco, CA 94108; 415-781-5180

FLORIDA
145 S.W. 107th Ave., Miami, FL 33174; 305-559-6715

HAWAII
1143 Bishop Street, Honolulu, HI 96813; 808-521-2731

ILLINOIS
172 North Michigan Ave., Chicago, IL 60601; 312-346-4228

LOUISIANA
4403 Veterans Memorial Blvd., Metairie, LA 70006; 504-887-7631

MASSACHUSETTS
50 St. Paul's Ave., Jamaica Plain, Boston, MA 02130; 617-522-8911
Rte. 1, 885 Providence Hwy., Dedham, MA 02026; 617-326-5385

MISSOURI
9804 Watson Rd., St. Louis, MO 63126; 314-965-3512

NEW JERSEY
561 U.S. Route 1, Wick Plaza, Edison, NJ 08817; 908-572-1200

NEW YORK
150 East 52nd Street, New York, NY 10022; 212-754-1110
78 Fort Place, Staten Island, NY 10301; 718-447-5071

OHIO
2105 Ontario Street, Cleveland, OH 44115; 216-621-9427

PENNSYLVANIA
9171-A Roosevelt Blvd., Philadelphia, PA
19114; 215-676-9494

SOUTH CAROLINA
243 King Street, Charleston, SC 29401; 803-577-0175

TENNESSEE
4811 Poplar Ave., Memphis, TN 38117; 901-761-2987

TEXAS
114 Main Plaza, San Antonio, TX 78205; 210-224-8101

VIRGINIA
1025 King Street, Alexandria, VA 22314; 703-549-3806

CANADA
3022 Dufferin Street, Toronto, Ontario, Canada M6B 3T5; 416-781-9131
1155 Yonge Street, Toronto, Ontario, Canada M4T 1W2; 416-934-3440